Pray, Write, Grow

Cultivating Prayer and Writing Together

ED CYZEWSKI

Pray, Write, Grow: Cultivating Prayer and Writing Together

By Ed Cyzewski

2015
Copyright © Ed Cyzewski, All Rights Reserved

Front Cover Design by Renee Malloy Ludlam
http://www.reneemalloyludlam.com/

* * *

**Learn about new releases and get discounts on future books
by joining Ed's e-newsletter!
Visit www.edcyzewski.com today!**

TABLE OF CONTENTS

INTRODUCTION

Every time you bow your head in prayer, open up a blank document on your computer, or flip open a journal page to write, you're taking a leap of faith. Writers choose to believe they can string together another series of sentences that will speak to the needs of readers somewhere. When people pray, they're choosing to believe there's a good, loving God reaching out to us, listening to our prayers, and meeting with us.

We have faith that the discipline of writing will pay off. If we keep working at it, keep practicing, keep asking for feedback, keep revising, and keep publishing our work wherever possible, we'll get better, reach more readers, and take meaningful steps forward. If we face the most challenging and vulnerable parts of our lives, we have faith that we'll find words that offer clarity and perspective. If we put our words in front of readers, we have faith that some will reply, "Yes! Me too!" If we take the time to continually examine ourselves and care for ourselves, we have faith that the words will continue to come together year in, year out, whatever life throws at us.

We have faith that the practices of silence, praying with scripture, or reciting the prayers passed on to us will bear fruit over time. If we continue to fight through our fears and anxieties in order to sit in silence, we trust that God can meet us, even if it leads to results we aren't expecting or doesn't even result in quantifiable progress. If we continue to cultivate habits of stillness and quiet throughout the day, we have faith that God can meet us and will speak even at moments when we aren't expecting to hear anything. If we continue to wait on God, we have faith that periods of silence don't indicate God has abandoned us.

We can even have faith that growing in one practice could lead to growth in the other.

Every time I grow as a writer, my prayer time receives direction. Every time I grow in my prayer time, my writing has increased clarity.

Writing and prayer stand well enough on their own, but many of the disciplines that help you write better will also help you pray better and vise versa. This wasn't something I planned out. I never set out to find connections between the two. Rather, I spend significant parts of each day writing and praying, and at a certain point I started to notice how the two converged. As I prayed, my writing started to shift and grow. Both the disciplines of prayer and the lessons I learned transferred over to my writing, and my writing furthered my personal reflection and helped foster the habits and disciplines I'd been cultivating while praying. When prayer and writing finally started working together in my life, I began to take significant steps forward in both simultaneously. Ironically, I finally saw all of this most clearly while doing neither.

A few years ago I started taking walks with our firstborn son most mornings so that he could nap. We walked nearly every bitter cold winter day with him. I bundled him up in a stroller sleeping sack and a snow suit. He could sleep for one or two hours most days, and I acutely felt the drain on my writing and prayer time. While I typically listened to podcasts during our walks, I began to question the wisdom of this. I had so much work to do. Perhaps I didn't need to listen to podcasts for the entire walk. What if I could use some of the walk to think of writing topics? At the very least I could sit down to write with some fresh ideas scribbled in a pocket notebook.

And if the writing ideas didn't come together, I reasoned that I could recite some prayers. The Jesus Prayer is perfect for filling in time with its simplicity: "Jesus Christ, Son of God, have mercy on me, a sinner." I could also meditate on the scripture verses from the morning office, one of a series of prayers and readings known as "The Hours" or "The Divine Hours" that follow the liturgical calendar and have been practiced by Christians for centuries. The possibilities were endless, really. Almost every Christian I know has said at one point or another, "I don't pray enough." What if my walks could become havens for prayer each day?

Such plans always start with enthusiasm and optimism, but despair quickly begins to take hold. While this plan sounds perfectly sensible in retrospect, I'd been listening to podcasts "religiously" every single day at that point in my life. They were "essential" for my walks. I love podcasts. It's like taking the best of the radio and the internet with you wherever you go. Habits and love for entertainment aside, there was something far worse lingering in the back of my mind--something that I didn't even fully realize until the first time I turned my iPod off and left my headphones in my pocket during a walk.

I'd been using podcasts to avoid being alone with my own thoughts. Podcasts were just one of the many tools I'd been using to avoid self-reflection. As soon as I started walking without podcasts playing, my mind exploded with worry and fear. I can't even say that I was fully aware of this happening. The habits of anxiety and worry simply kicked in as soon as I had some free space in my mind. The podcasts had been one of my strategies for keeping my worries at bay.

Those first few days of trying to walk without podcasts were torture. Some days I caved after a few minutes. Other days I endured the silence of my thoughts for about 30 minutes before flipping my iPod on. I tried to focus on praying. I tried to focus on writing ideas. Instead my mind just spun out of control. I couldn't focus on much of anything. It was a disaster. Before giving up, I tried to make bargains with myself. I finally decided that I couldn't stand being in my own head for an entire walk. The podcasts became a reward on the way home if I could endure the first half of the walk.

This incentive kept me going. I faced my chaotic thoughts every morning. Over time the dread of those walks began to dissipate. In fact, I started to realize that the things I'd been obsessively worrying over were legitimate writing and prayer topics. Soon I began jotting down notes in a pocket notebook or tapping ideas on my phone's note app. At the same time I began opening up about my anxieties and fears to God in prayer. After writing a note, I often prayed about that particular thing, offering my problems to God and then letting my mind wander wherever. Sometimes I reached clarity on a particular issue, and the more I inched toward clarity, the more I had to write about.

I don't know why I stuck with it at first. Perhaps I was desperate enough to try something different. As I created space for my mind to unwind during my walks, I started to see what I needed to pray and write about. The more I walked, the more I craved that quiet time to pray and to think of writing topics. I started to recognize unhealthy signs, such as my mind spinning on and on about a problem at work or an issue in my personal life. The constant motion of life had fostered an anxiety breeding ground where I was running from one thing to another, constantly worrying about every little detail and never fully resolving anything because there was something else to worry about even more.

The more I used walks to create space in my mind for prayer and writing, the more I began to value that time. I stopped dreading the first 45 minutes of my walk. In fact, I started having so many things to think and pray about that I started skipping the podcasts on my walk home. Today I can't even tell you when I last listened to a podcast during my daily walk. And I assure you, this is not driven by any kind of superhuman discipline on my part. It took a lot of discipline and agony to keep the podcasts turned off at first, but at this point, it's now a habit to keep my walks open as free mental space for prayer and writing ideas. It's something that I do without even thinking about it.

I leave the house, and I let my mind wander and spin through whatever comes up. If I'm worried, I face those thoughts and leave myself open to pray about them or reflect on whether there's something to write about. By the time I've finished a walk, I have often uncovered at least one thing that I really need to sort out through writing, prayer, or both. When I miss a walk, I feel the strain of losing that free mental space. Praying and thinking during my walks are no longer disciplines that I have to force myself to do. They are habits that I've practiced long enough to see real rewards that motivate me to be stay the course.

Those walks finally shut down that negative loop of anxiety and despair and introduced me to a different loop where I could pray and write. I suspect that both prayer and writing can offer a lot of benefits by themselves. I certainly don't think you have to do them together. However, if you're already inclined to both write and pray, you may as well figure out how they can help each other. And if you're experienced in one, you may find opportunities for personal or spiritual growth by trying out the other. I would even go so far as saying it like this:

If you want to improve your prayer life, try writing.

If you want to improve your writing life, try praying.

The two require many of the same practices, disciplines, and virtues. Of course you should certainly only pray out of an interest to meet with God on a deeper level, just as you should only write if you have something to say or process. I'm not trying to tap into the commercial writing potential for prayer or to guilt the reluctant into writing. Rather, I want to drive home the point that prayer and writing not only happily co-exist, but also feed off of each other and can benefit each other.

When I talk about prayer, it could be anything from petitioning God with specific requests, to engaging in the discipline of the Examen, to silent practices such as centering prayer or quiet meditation. When I talk about writing it could be anything from journaling privately, to self-publishing, to publishing commercially. Whether you write fiction or nonfiction, blog regularly, or jot notes in a little journal, the practice of writing requires observation and processing that enables writers to see the truth with greater clarity.

If you feel called to pray more, writing will help sort out your thoughts. If you feel called to write more, perhaps you should figure out how to pray in order to expose the topics you need to write about and what you should write. If you struggle at one, I wouldn't be surprised to learn that you also struggle with the other since both call us to a lifestyle of observation and self-reflection, which are two things that are hard to do in our distraction-filled world.

This intersection of prayer and writing is the kind of thing I should have noticed a lot sooner. I've been writing professionally either part time or full time since 2005, which also happens to be the year I graduated from seminary with a Master of Divinity degree and zero interest in working at a church.

Now, if you spoke to someone who, say, attended dental hygiene school for four years but had no intention of coming near anyone's teeth after graduating, you'd probably have some questions. You may ask, "Don't you know your degree is basically useless if you don't work with teeth?" About halfway through seminary, I realized that I really didn't want to work in the church as a pastor. I had a scholarship, so I figured I may as well finish, but I didn't really have much of a plan B in the works.

In the back of my mind I had this vague notion that I'd one day write something--perhaps a book. During my final semester of seminary, I drafted a book with the guidance of a professor, and against all odds published that book with two study guides in 2008. A little bit of success meant that writing became my plan B, and I've been living at the intersection of faith and writing ever since. If you live in both of these worlds as well, I hope this book will help you take a few steps toward sorting out the relationship between them.

So far, I've narrowed it down to this: pray, write, grow. There isn't a flow chart or a how-to system to it. I can't tell you if you're "doing it right." It's a gradual process of growth. If you're new to a practice such as centering prayer or the Examen, they will most certainly feel like "work" at first. As you cultivate strengths such as awareness of your surroundings and yourself, you'll find that there's quite a lot to pray and write about. If you keep that loop of prayer and writing going, you'll most certainly grow. Perhaps you'll grow more in one practice than the other, but intentionally pursuing both at the same time can create powerful momentum.

We have a tendency at times to erect barriers between the "sacred" and the "secular." For writers, especially writers of faith,* such barriers can hold them back both professionally and spiritually. By seeing the connections between prayer and writing, we'll take leaps forward in both, overcome perceived barriers, and even discover new paths that we may have overlooked.

At the 2012 STORY conference, author and writing instructor Anne Lamott shared, "Everything I know about prayer also applies to writing. And everything I know about writing also applies to prayer." I just about jumped out of my seat and shouted, "Yes!" Mind you, she communicated everything I said above in two sentences, but that's why people pay her to speak at conferences.

You could have literally dropped her talk about writing at a creativity conference, into a conference dedicated to developing prayer practices. It's uncanny, really. If you're a writer and a person of faith, this is extremely good news. However, while there are many benefits to this approach, the process will not be easy.

The Cost of Writing and Prayer

I don't claim to have the secret solution to your every struggle with prayer or writing. Actually, a lot of what I'm about to share could be perceived by some as "bad news" or least some hard truths. There aren't short cuts to either of these practices, and if you want to develop in one, you have to make some steep sacrifices at times. This book is a bit like a frank talk that I often have with friends and colleagues interested in breaking into the Christian publishing field.

First off: This is going to HURT. There are tremendous rewards, but there's a cost and the rewards you end up receiving may not be the rewards you have in mind at the beginning. Speaking from my own experience, I've found that I don't even end up missing the things I had once fought tooth and nail to give up. I don't miss my podcasts when I take walks these days because the mental space that walks create is so beneficial.

I hope this book provides a reality check for the costs and benefits of taking your prayer and writing more seriously. If prayer and writing both succeed for many of the same reasons, they also can fail for many of the same reasons.

Children can provide no end of interruptions and zap the life force out of us.

Family drama can dig into our schedules and our mental energy.

Social media, sports, gossip, and the 24-hour news cycle can suck up time, perpetuate anxiety, and clog valuable space in our minds.

Guilt about failing to follow through can leave us frustrated and unable to begin again.

Self-doubt will lead to one false start after another.

Fear can send us reeling at any moment.

We have to face each of these obstacles and overcome them. We have to make sacrifices, ask hard questions, and look into the most wounded parts of ourselves in order to fight our way to the other side.

This is challenging, and we can't make progress by dabbling in either practice. Sometimes we have to give up on the good in order to reach the best. Sometimes limitations lead to greater freedom. Sometimes things have to get worse before they get better.

If you want to grow as a writer and a person of prayer, there are real, practical steps you can take. You can become a better writer. You can overcome the obstacles that keep you from praying and writing.

As you progress in both prayer and writing, you'll gain greater clarity on yourself and the direction of your life. You'll be able to spot your vices and virtues. You'll have wisdom to share and discover ways you can help others. Over time you may gain clarity into your passions and dreams so that you can better focus how you spend your time. Writing and prayer don't solve our every problem, but they can help us take some positive steps forward and take us to a place where we can meet with God and serve others.

If you're willing to make some sacrifices, you can start moving forward. We begin with the step that makes everything after it possible.

*One little disclaimer at the beginning: I'm writing this book from the Christian tradition here, and if you're unaffiliated or a member of a different faith, I'll just warn you upfront that I can only write out of what I have experienced. I'm not trying to trick anyone into becoming a Christian with this book. However, if you've been hesitant to pray or find prayer difficult, I hope that I can provide some concrete steps forward, even if they come from a tradition other than your own.

CHAPTER ONE

CREATING SPACE TO PRAY AND WRITE

Subtraction Must Precede Addition

Spiritual director Larry Warner shared in a workshop in 2014 that every addition to our lives requires a subtraction. If you're trying to add something to your life without subtracting something else, there's a good chance the stuff that's already there will win. Old habits are tenacious and can rob us of any hope that our lives could change or improve.

On the one hand, that sounds like a no-brainer. However, I have seen this struggle of over-commitment over and over again. For instance, not too long ago I noticed in my daily Examen that I was staying up too late, struggling to get up early enough to get my day going, and rarely finding enough time to write and pray. I just needed more resolve to go to bed early, right?

After crashing and burning for a month or two, I realized that while I struggled with resolve and discipline, I often stayed up late because I was doing laundry, dishes, or another household project. Once I'd already stayed up late on these projects, I often wanted to unwind a little, and that's what killed me. I could stay up an extra hour just because I wanted to relax after doing housework. I also noticed that some nights I may just need to sacrifice some sleep in order to keep up with things around the house.

As a result, I've changed two things about my day. For starters, I try to be a little more proactive about chores such as the dishes and laundry during the day. If I can steal a few minutes here and there, I try to remember that every minute saved earlier in the day will pay off in the evening. I also try to give myself a bit of a break when I need to stay up late. It's not always a failure of my will if I need to go to bed late. Sometimes you can't add an early bed time if you'd like to keep the laundry from piling up in the basement or the dishes from cascading out of the sink.

While we can all tinker with our commitments and schedules, perhaps the most important thing is to recognize the importance of prayer and writing. They need to be at the top of our daily lists. If you can only manage to complete four out of six things on your daily to-do list, prioritize prayer and writing to make sure you get them done first if at all possible. While this isn't something everyone can or even should do, if you feel called to write or you desire to improve your prayer life, you'll need to make some sacrifices in order to prioritize both. If you start to make room for prayer and writing, you'll also, hopefully, start to see enough benefits to continue making space for them.

Perhaps we'll be most motivated to make the necessary sacrifices to pray and write if we keep some goals or outcomes in mind. For instance, prayer and writing may relieve anxiety, provide direction for our lives, and connect us with like-minded people. Perhaps you can point out people you would like to imitate because they are wise, accomplished, merciful, or kind to others, but you can't figure out how you could even come close to resembling them. While we should never get lost in the comparison game since we each have our own callings and talents, our approach to writing and prayer can help us take meaningful steps out of despair and aimlessness. In fact, writing and prayer can help us tap into our God-given passions that will help us serve others and lead fulfilling lives. We'll get to that later in this book. For now, we need to lay the ground work for writing and prayer: making space to pray and write.

Before we look at "adding" more prayer or writing practices into our lives, we have to begin with "subtraction." This is where the costs of writing and prayer come into sharper focus before we can develop the practices that will help us move forward into new territory. Our lives are often cluttered with so many thoughts, activities, and practices that are either neutral or slightly detrimental without being "bad" for us. Sometimes we have very good things in our lives that have taken up an unhealthy amount of space. However you want to classify these things, we need subtract the things that make it difficult to add prayer and writing to our lives. Skipping this step will only lead to frustration and give yourself the false impression that you're not good at prayer and writing or that you're "too busy." Anyone can pray or write, but few make the time for either.

We'll be able to pray and write more effectively when we learn to create physical space for both, block out time in our schedules so that both become habits, and give ourselves mental space for both to happen naturally. In other words, we don't have to necessarily try harder in order to improve at prayer or writing. The majority of us are too cluttered, distracted, stressed, and busy to do either well in the first place. Before we try harder, we have to look at how we spend our time each day. All of the tips and training in the world related to prayer and writing won't help us if we're not committed to making room for them in our daily schedules.

And while we're talking about Larry Warner, he also suggests that we use the word "full" rather than "busy" to discuss our day-to-day schedules. The word "busy" can carry a connotation of self-importance and even uncontrollable chaos. More to our purposes here, the idea of being busy could lead to despair, while the idea of being full presents a ready solution. We don't know how to "un-busy" ourselves, but we can imagine how to "un-fill" ourselves. Those who are too "full" need to dump out the non-essentials in order to create more space to add prayer and writing.

Physical Space to Pray and Write

Experts in writing and prayer both note that a dedicated space for either practice can be revolutionary. When you sit down in a particular chair or kneel in a particular location, you need to know what happens next.

Neither will thrive if you plop down on the couch where you usually watch television. And if the television is still on, then don't even bother trying.

I have lived in several different places since I started writing seriously, and in each home I developed habits and routines that centered around specific locations where I would pray and write. You may benefit from reading *The Power of Habit* by Charles Duhigg. While Duhigg writes for a business audience--which also has the most disposable income--he effectively distills key insights from researchers related to habits. For instance, when you sit down to write, do you typically check your email or visit a social media page? If you do that every time, that's a habit. What if you could create the same kind of habit for prayer? What if you knew exactly what needed to happen next once you sat down in a particular spot? Something like that had happened to me without even realizing it.

Early in our marriage we bought a red couch and matching red chair from a yard sale. Besides really loving to sit in that red chair in the morning with my coffee, I started to pray the hours there every day. In fact, I'd grown so attached to praying each morning in that particular red chair that I struggled to pray for a few weeks after we sold it during a cross-country move. I had no idea why prayer didn't click until I set aside a different place to pray each morning. As long as I had a spot dedicated to prayer at a particular time of day, I rarely struggled with distractions that could pull me off course. The same intentional use of space has proven critical for my writing.

After living in several homes and experimenting with several desk set ups, I have personally thrived by keeping my desk relatively spartan, only allowing clutter related to a specific project. I could be wrong about this, but all of this talk about creativity being fueled by clutter makes one big blunder for writers. Writers often let clutter from other areas of their lives invade their writing spaces. I won't argue with the psychologists who say that a messy work space encourages outside the box thinking, but clutter from areas other than your work could result in not getting any writing done. If you want to pile up notebooks, pens, pads, books serving as sources, and even typewriters in order to get yourself in the mood, have at it. However, when you pile up bills, broken toys from your kids, files from a different project, and dirty dishes in your writing space, you've only given yourself a pile of things to remind yourself of what you could be doing instead of writing. You may even convince yourself that these things are more important than writing in the heat of the moment--especially when you get stuck on a tough paragraph.

These days I usually write in a cafe since its free from kids and household work, but if I do write at home, my desk is always clear of mail, dishes, unrelated books, and anything else that could prove distracting. I have a higher shelf with some helpful books, a desk lamp, and a frame with some pictures of my kids, but I still have a pretty huge open space where I can write in my journal or on a computer. I'll gladly pile up relevant books or notepads, but unnecessary sticky notes, computer stuff, and random bits of paper are all hidden out of sight. If it's warm outside, I prefer to write on our front porch where I'm surrounded by flowers that I plant each Spring.

A simple question may help you think about your desk space: Is this helping me write?

This kind of question can be generalized about any environment where we are trying to write or pray: Is this place or practice helping me or holding me back? We could ask questions like: Will a walk give me more mental space to pray or write? Do I need more time to free write in my journal? Sometimes the answer may change depending on the time of day or the day of the week.

While prayer can be practiced at any point of the day, the time we need for quiet meditation and identifying the areas God needs to work on will be best spent in quiet, or at least keeping ourselves silent since we can't control what others say or do if we're walking. A quiet moment in the early morning or late evening can also create a space that is conducive for prayer. I've often prayed while walking, but the details aren't as important as long as your attention is fully given to God in the moment. Sometimes we have to just cry out for help in the midst of a chaotic day and our prayer stops there. Other times we can walk and let our minds wander wherever God may lead. And still other times we let questions, scripture, or the prayers of others guide us into a greater awareness of God's presence.

While the atmosphere we foster for writing or prayer won't guarantee focused prayer or productive writing, I've found that it's at least important to recognize how our environments impact our writing and prayer. Now that we have two kids, I really crave a morning walk just to give myself a little bit of time to ponder some writing ideas or to pray. Our toddler munches on snacks while our newborn naps. I suspect these peaceful walks will soon give way to less focused outings once our older son is ready to ride a bike!

I don't expect everyone to create routines that replicate my own. I understand every person has different limitations and each season of life offers unique challenges. We can't control everything about the places we pray or write. Some days are easier to control than others. But if you can control even a small space at home for your writing, take walks, or find a third place, you'll at least give yourself a better shot at focused prayer or reflection for writing.

Perhaps a local church or cathedral offers a peaceful atmosphere for prayer. I know some friends who light candles every week while praying, using the flame as a reminder of God's presence in the midst of their requests. Many writers thrive by going out to a public spot just to be around other people who are productive. If I don't show up at my local café after more than a week, the baristas assume that I'm dead.

Scheduling Space to Pray and Write

We all have a schedule each day whether or not we've written up an agenda on a physical calendar or calendar app. To a certain degree my schedule is at the mercy of my children and has evolved over time depending on when they go to sleep and wake up. My wife and I spend time at the start of her semesters to plan our schedules together, ensuring we both get enough time to meet our goals. As each season of life brings new changes, I've been able to adapt my schedule in order to make prayer and writing more likely to happen than not.

For instance, if I can count on my son to sleep in until 7:00 am or later most mornings, I can go to bed early and wake up in time to pray the hours and write a little before he wakes up. I can also find little windows of time throughout the day, such as the time after a walk where at least one of my kids wants to play by himself and I have five to ten minutes to pray the afternoon office.

Each evening before bed I make a point of praying the Compline and completing the Ignatian Examen. The Examen is a series of directed meditations and questions that help us put into words the good and the bad aspects of our days. However, the catch is that sometimes the things I note as "good" are actually problems, and the things I consider "bad" actually turn into opportunities for growth and redemption.

I usually work through the Examen each evening using an iPhone app (called "Examine"), but there are plenty of guides you can find online if you want to print it out or transfer it into a journal. The app I use begins with a series of reminders about God's presence and then asks whether you're discouraged or encouraged. It follows with a series of "consonance" questions about what's going well in your life and then a series of "dissonance" questions about what's not going well. It ends with an invitation to meditate for five minutes or to share your thoughts with a friend or spiritual director.

I've been praying the Hours and the Examen long enough that they are both habits, and even if I forget my prayer book or iPad, which has both loaded on the front screen, I can work through the key parts of both from memory. These prayer practices aren't just scheduled. They're essential habits that feel like integral parts of my day. I often sleep better after praying the hours and the Examen, so I'm especially motivated to keep both in my daily routine.

When I schedule time to write, I know that I'll either sit at my desk, front porch in the summer, or in a local café. As often as our schedules allow, I try to give myself blocks of three to four hours straight so that I have enough time to keep my personal projects and client work going.

Focusing your scheduled time on a specific task is much like keeping your physical space limited to your work. You'll only be distracted and less effective while multi-tasking. Single-minded focus in your space and schedule is the key to making progress in both prayer and writing. Without a dedicated block that immediately prompts you to begin writing or praying for a set period of time, you'll always find a distraction.

I've found it immensely helpful to set timers for both prayer and writing. The "Examine" app comes with a five-minute meditation buzzer that notifies you when your time is up. I use programs like Freedom and SelfControl to work in 30-minute blocks on my writing without online distractions.

Small wins will make a huge difference in writing and prayer, so don't overlook the importance of completing relatively small goals and then building on them. Learning to meditate in silence for five minutes is no small task for many in our loud culture. Your life will change in unexpected ways when you manage to take control of even five minutes.

You can get a ton of writing done if you wake up even 30 minutes early since you'll have fewer distractions. I have only seen diminishing returns by staying up late to work. I have always been more productive by going to bed at a reasonable time and waking up early if I need to gain ground on a writing project. The added bonus of waking up early to write is that a quiet house is also a great place to pray!

Mental Space to Pray and Write

There's only so much time in a day, and any time I devote to thinking about, for instance, a sports team, means I have that much less time to pray or write. I felt this conflict acutely when I tried to write on the side while working full time.

I needed to make the most of my free time during lunch, in the morning, and on the weekend to write. That urgency has only grown as I try to balance time with my children and freelance writing work.

I have learned that I need more than my dedicated writing and prayer time in order to thrive at both. I needed to create an atmosphere where both could happen at any moment in short bursts--even bursts of a few seconds at a time. Sometimes ideas need time to take shape while washing the dishes, or prayers can form while folding laundry. I needed my prayer and writing time to function more like a continuation of what has already been going on in my spirit and mind. I needed raw materials in hand before taking on some focused time for both. This meant that I had to eliminate the extra noise in my life.

While I don't want to make it sound like I never watch television shows or listen to the radio or podcasts, I've made some major changes to how I spend my time.

For instance, I used to watch sports every evening and weekend. I used to play the radio while doing the dishes and driving to work. I've already mentioned that I used to load up the latest podcasts for walks. Entertainment, news, and cultural programming have their places for sure, but I had filled every single empty moment of my life with someone talking.

My mind hardly had any time to process life. I was living in a constant state of information consumption and didn't give myself a chance to process anything either by way of prayer or writing. Breaking free from the constant chatter of podcasts was difficult, but that was only the beginning. I started creating more "empty mental space" throughout my days, and my mind unraveled as I obsessed over everything that wasn't going well in my life. I worried and stressed and felt like everything was crumbling around me. Of course things weren't that bad, but given a little free time, my mind began worrying in overdrive.

I started to recognize that these struggles with anxiety during quiet moments served as symptoms of a bigger problem. I had been medicating my anxiety with distractions and noise. More experiments followed: I began flipping off the radio in the kitchen and in the car. I cut back on the sports I watched in the evenings and weekends. I tried to strike a balance with entertainment and created space for my mind and spirit.

While I can't say this is ideal for everyone, I also avoided almost all news except for one or two non-sensational written sources. Some news stations specialize in sensationalizing what's less important or focus only on the negative events of the day. I have completely removed myself from all televised news. I am still aware of elections and donate to charity and remain a "member of society." However, the 24-hour news cycle has been quite toxic for me personally. I don't think I'm any less engaged with local politics or local charities by avoiding televised news. I encourage everyone to pick a cause or two and to devote themselves to it, but the constant consumption of televised news focuses on soundbites and thumbnail summaries rather than the careful analysis you can find in written news reports from expert sources.

I can't tell you what's best for you, but speaking for myself, I often noticed that watching the news left me stressed out and hopeless. I would get all worked up over some issue based on a 30 or 60-second story and spend the next hour obsessing over it. If you factored in a dispute on social media, I could devote even more time and energy to it. Being informed about today's critical issues is excellent, but feeling stressed out and hopeless will prevent you from taking meaningful action that could make a difference, let alone be present for your family, work, and spiritual practices. This may not be a big deal for you, but as I've taken stock of my soul over the years, I've found that changing my sources for news has made a huge difference in my outlook each day.

If I don't have some quiet moments during a walk, I try to at least give myself some quiet while doing the dishes or sorting the laundry. Watering the garden or putting clothes away can offer a valuable span of time to get my mind and spirit in order. In fact, the chores I used to dread became havens of for my mind and spirit. I started to view these dull, repetitive chores as opportunities to let my mind wander for prayer or pondering a writing topic. If I've had some time to reflect, think, and pray throughout the day, then I feel free to tune in to a podcast or hockey game in the evening.

It's not a precise science. It's more a matter of taking your mental or spiritual temperature. If my mind is overheating with stress and worry, it's usually because I haven't taken time to process everything that has been spinning out of control in both my conscious mind and even subconsciousness.

Giving myself more mental "space" has enabled me to identify the unhealthy stuff that I've been obsessing over--the stuff that feeds my constant anxiety. A bit of mental space makes it possible to ask if I've devoted too much time to the latest bit of drama among my online friends. Perhaps I'm worried about my next freelance project. Perhaps I need to think through a theological issue that has been disturbing me. Each of these reflections have provided direction for my writing and my prayer.

If something is causing stress, then I should pray about it. And if an issue has been eating at me for a while, there's a good chance it's eating at someone else who would be relieved to read about my process should I write about it.

I often jot down ideas after a walk or after praying in the evening. After I've written about them the following day, I'll usually have greater clarity during the following evening when I pray.

Putting It All Together

Writing and prayer don't happen by accident. We don't just stumble into them. We have to cut things out of our lives, make sacrifices, and give ourselves the mental, physical, and scheduled spaces where they can take root and thrive. Prayer and writing need a place in our lives to take root before they can flourish. Cutting out the distractions and noise that prevent us from both practices can be disruptive and challenging at first. It's hard to admit that something as insignificant as a news story, podcast, or social media post has prevented you from praying or writing. However, if you're struggling to find time for prayer and writing, this is where you need to begin.

The good news is that you won't have to struggle quite so much to write and pray as you engage in both practices regularly. You'll start to develop routines and habits that will make both significantly easier to do. When you sit down to write, you'll know that it's time to check your notes from yesterday's walk or the previous evening's prayers so that you can start writing. When you take a walk, your mind will welcome the space to pray and ponder whatever's been on your mind. As you engage in both practices on a routine basis, you'll start to grow and to see how much they benefit you. You'll enjoy the clarity and direction both provide. While you will surely struggle to focus when praying sometimes, and you'll certainly need to write many drafts when working on a writing project, the progress you make will eventually become its own reward. You'll feel the peace of prayer and the satisfaction of writing regularly.

You may even start to notice when you haven't had enough time to pray or write.

Without recognizing the ways we waste time and/or mental energy, we'll struggle to pray and write in ways that are personally relevant, to say nothing of the benefits that could come to others.

28

CHAPTER TWO

LEARNING TO BE PRESENT

Where Do Writing and Prayer Begin?

I started eavesdropping on conversations against my will.

I spent my first four years as a freelance writer working in a cafe that was frequented by local high school students who became my unsuspecting tutors. I'd just graduated from seminary a few years earlier, and I'd picked up so much "academic-speak," that I'd lost touch with the average reader. As I worked on my first book project, I often slipped into highly technical theological jargon. The high school students provided writing prompts as I figured out how to write for the typical reader.

Most afternoons a table full of loud-talking students settled in my general vicinity, and inevitably one of them would shout something completely ridiculous. I'm sure it made sense in context. I'd jot down a sentence or two from these conversations as a writing prompt and begin to flesh out my own narrative.

While these students helped me to write a bit more like a normal person, my eavesdropping also taught me how to be fully present in the moment, to observe my surroundings and to listen to people. Writers often make the mistake of thinking that our ideas come when we sit down and face a blank page. That may happen, but I have found more often than not that a walk, visit to the store, or online conversation can provide some of my most important writing prompts.

For instance, I thought of one book project after talking with a couple of young adults about some negative church experiences. Another book project arose from a conversation with a church elder about the challenges he faced with a particular group of people.

We're already familiar enough with the idea of listening to someone for a prayer request, but our writing can be guided in a similar manner. In fact, people are always tweeting and posting about the things they worry about, struggle over, and find difficult. The people around us may reveal what we should write about.

However, we don't just pay attention to others. Our prayer and writing will be most effective when we tune in to both ourselves and other people. If you're ready to jot down a note or to ruminate on a conversation you've had with someone or overheard, you'll be prepared to write. If you are aware of what's bothering yourself or someone you know, you'll have something relevant and important to pray about.

Building the Right Foundation

Some may think that these suggestions are all well and good for me, but perhaps they fear immediate failure when sitting down to pray or write. What makes me so sure this could ever possibly work for anyone else?

Perhaps we don't know what to write or we fear what critical readers will think of our work. Perhaps we fear that God won't show up when we pray, and we don't know if that means there's something wrong with us or God simply isn't real.

When facing the uncertain starting points for prayer and writing, we can begin to view certain practices as almost magical or we can turn God into a genie who will only respond if we rub the bottle just right. We start to obsess over an inner "muse" for our writing. Others imagine that God has some petty grievance against vile sinners who dare to pray, thinking they need to get themselves straightened out. This leads to all kinds of bargaining and tricks to get either God or the muse to show up.

We try all kinds of writing prompts or buy special notebooks to jumpstart our writing. We recite special prayers or incorporate new rituals in order to woo God over to our sides.

I've certainly picked up cool notebooks for my writing, and I've recited certain prayers at times, but these are tools that can help us down the line after we've laid a solid foundation. They won't serve us well as the foundation itself.

We don't begin with writing or prayer by hanging everything on a particular trick, practice, or method. We begin with learning how to be present. In the words of Jesus, we need eyes to see and ears to hear. I mean that both metaphorically and literally. In fact, you already have everything you need to begin with prayer or writing. Anyone can accomplish either right now, whether or not you have a fancy notebook or expensive prayer book.

Being Present and Being Ourselves

Prayer and writing can happen at any time and any place. However, we won't be able to tap into the deeper life of prayer or the flow of writing if we haven't learned how to be present in the moment.

Ironically, both my Christian and non-religious friends may find this concept of being present either troubling or at least vague. For some Christians this idea of being "present" may sound a little too broad and tied to other belief systems, and for the non-religious it may sound a little too religious. It's true that many religions speak to this practice of being present, but the difference is what we do once we are present. We're just getting started when we talk about being present, but it is one of the most challenging practices for us today with all of the technology and entertainment surrounding us.

Think of it this way, when are you ever fully involved in one thing without any distractions or interruptions? I'll bet you often have a phone around that can start buzzing with alerts, text messages, or calls. If you're working on a computer, there's a good chance you have an Internet browser open. If you're home, there's always something else that can pull you away from prayer or writing. If you're just running an errand, it's easy to kill time here and there by checking email or social media on your smart phone.

We've already talked about removing these kinds of distractions from our lives in order to pray and write. Here is where we start to find a pay off.

Focused single-tasking means that when you walk down the street, you let your mind wander and simply observe what's around you. When you sit down to pray, you try to remove every distraction. Perhaps you use a scripture verse or brief prayer to focus your mind.

If you're praying, take steps to be fully present for prayer, such as closing your eyes, finding a quiet spot without distractions, or walking in order to remove any temptation to seek distractions. If you're writing, close down everything else on your computer that isn't helping you write. Use a journal or notepad to jot down ideas, free write, or draft a project. Turn off your phone if you can. Most importantly, being present means we stop multi-tasking and start asking what it looks like to be fully aware of a specific moment.

This will be a struggle at first. In fact, you may need time to figure out what it means for you to be fully present in a particular moment. Many writers I know say that they need as much as thirty minutes of free writing in a journal or editing yesterday's work before they're fully able to focus on their work for the day. By the same token, it often takes me a bit of time to calm myself and focus on prayer.

Learning to See Each Day

Stopping and focusing is hard enough, but as we begin to sort out the particulars of being present for writing and prayer, we'll begin to see the world differently. We'll find peace in prayer as we begin to rest in God's presence rather than constantly measuring our experiences or progress. Our writing will also become less frantic as we focus on the single project before us--even if we can only write for 30-60 minutes at a time. This is a process that will have its share of setbacks and struggles along the way. However, if we're practicing being fully present, we'll prepare ourselves for prayer and creative work throughout each day.

When I started praying the Examen, which asks a series of questions about my day, I struggled to answer the question that prompted me to identify a point when I felt God's presence. Some days I sensed God's presence, but on other days prayer felt like merely reciting words and waiting in silence. I didn't have anything in particular I could nail down as a moment when God felt particularly present.

That started to change when I prayed with my young son one evening. After my wife and I read books with him, we started taking turns to pray with him before saying goodnight. Turning the lights off, I usually kneel down next to his bed where he's tucked in and eager to share everything he's thankful for. We usually begin with saying thank you for things like his friends, family, church, and the local children's science museum. He's also thanked God for "daddy's shirt," "people watching hockey," and "mama holding brother." After he's exhausted every possible thing and person he could thank God for, I pray for him.

The prayers are always short because he's a toddler with a limited attention span, but the first time we prayed together, I sensed an immediate connection with God. It was as if God wanted to love my son through me, and that act of loving my son also opened me to a greater sense of God's parental love. The simple ritual of praying with my son eventually opened my eyes to a deeper sense of God's love for me and my love for my son.

I started noticing that prayer wasn't just a matter of saying thank you or issuing requests, even if it could be those things. Prayer gets us on the same page with God. It shifts our perspectives. I saw how God loves me and loves my son. My eyes were opened to the possibility that God could be found in other moments too. In fact, many of the moments I've spent with my children since that epiphany while praying have led to particularly powerful experiences of God's presence when I least expected it. Responding to my children with mercy or compassion became a kind of prayer in and of itself.

As I prayed through each of the questions in my Examen each evening, I started to recognize God's presence in the moments when I loved my children. For all of the times I'd sat down with prayer books or tried to quiet my mind to meditate on scripture, God felt most present while I spent time with my kids, whether praying or playing. The more I see God in these relationships with my children, the more I've become aware of how easily we can wall God's presence off from very important areas of our lives.

I am learning that God wants prayer in my life to evolve and spread throughout my daily practices, to learn that prayer can happen at any moment. I'm starting to see how God wants to connect with me throughout my day. I have also learned how my friends have had profound connections with God while cooking a meal for neighbors or nursing a child in the still of the evening. Each of these simple acts can create a point of connection with God. I don't know how we can "make" those connections happen, as I'm sure each person is different. Rather, we have to be aware that God is present throughout our days and is reaching out to us. It's no mistake that I struggled to experience God throughout my day when I wasn't even expecting God to show up, save for very limited and specific moments. In fact, the language of "God showing up" implies that we may even think that God isn't present and sometimes decides to show up. God is always present. We can't chant special words to make God appear. However, we can practice being present and aware of God's presence.

That isn't to say that playing with kids or cooking a meal always results in a profound moment of prayer or a sense of God's presence. Rather, we can be aware that God is present and could meet with us in these kinds of everyday moments if we train ourselves to be aware of this possibility. I have always loved my son, but I didn't always see how that love could relate to the way I prayed. As I started tuning into God's presence during my time with him, our play times became a sort of prayer.

In the same way, my daily life has provided no end of writing topics. There's always something to write about. Simply learning awareness in the moment has opened my eyes to many new directions for my writing. Particular moments throughout my day offer plenty of directions for my writing. I can ask why I'm repulsed by or drawn to a particular person. I can ask why I'm frustrated with my child. I can ask why I'm worried by a particular situation. I can explore the consequences of an action. Just stopping to take stock of my thoughts for a few moments can dig up many directions for my writing.

As I practiced awareness and presence throughout my days as a parent of young children, I realized that my greatest struggle most days was frustration when my children cry. It wasn't just annoyance at their behavior. It's something bigger, and as I worked on my Examen each evening, I started to see that my anger had a lot to do with control. I wanted to control how my children behaved, and if they started to cry, I wanted to be able to change the situation. However, sometimes babies are just fussy, and oftentimes toddlers are illogical or at least beyond reasoning. When the crying spirals out of control, I may as well join them on the floor, pounding my feet too.

These struggles with control weren't just something to pray about. I began writing about my battles with control and anger. These are the very topics that many parents can relate to. In the world of Christian writing, it's also particularly relevant to write about struggles with control and frustration when we're supposed to live by faith as we trust God with providing our daily bread.

I've also learned to be aware of what others are mentioning on social media and in my real life social groups. For instance, some of my most popular blog posts have addressed issues related to career planning, career failures, and fear of the future for young adults. While I have plenty of experience with switching careers and carving out a new path that has been filled with frustration and fear, I didn't think to write about any of this until I saw the tweets of a few twenty-something friends who are in the midst of graduate school and aren't sure about what the future holds. While I didn't mention them specifically in what I wrote, I directly addressed their fears and concerns.

I'm sure you've noticed a fine line here. Social media, for instance, can be both a blessing and curse to writers. On the one hand we can tap into never-ending drama and nit picking fights. Social media provides tremendous distraction. On the other we can tap into the real issues that people care about. The greatest difference is whether we're turning to something like social media in order to become more aware or to avoid our deeper issues.

As I practice presence and awareness, I usually jot down notes in a document in my journal, smart phone, or tablet throughout the day. Sometimes I'll dog-ear a page in my journal if I need to follow up on a book or article idea. When I sit down to write, I often have a fairly long list of potential topics to explore right off the bat in my note file or journal. Many ideas that struck me as "can't miss" topics when I jotted them down immediately fizzle when I try to write a paragraph based on my prompt. It's not a sure thing each and every time.

We are surrounded by writing and prayer prompts, but if we're always checking our phones or worrying about the latest dust up on social media, we'll cut ourselves off from them. In fact, I wrote and edited this chapter with Freedom cutting off my access to the internet. If it hadn't been for Freedom, I would have stopped working on this chapter to report on Facebook that a woman just elaborately posed her dog at a cafe table with a drink in order to take a picture. Who knows what would have happened after I posted that once my friends started commenting! It's likely that I wouldn't have written very much for at least the next fifteen minutes.

The Process of Learning to Be Present

As you take steps to carve out time for prayer and writing, don't let yourself fall into the trap of guilt or anxiety when you struggle to meet goals. I trust that you won't progress fast enough by your own measures, but this is a slow process. You can't expect life-changing growth to occur overnight. These are practices that we develop over time, and our prayer and writing will gradually change as we cultivate them. If you know anything about gardening, you should know that it's a slow process that demands months of work and waiting before yielding results.

The speed and stimulation of our culture is addicting. The acts of prayer and writing run counter to both. They both thrive in focus, silence, and presence, while our culture thrives in constant noise and is always freaking out about the next thing that often hasn't even happened yet.

You may need to set alarms on your phone as a reminder to check in and take stock of your mental or spiritual state. You may need to carry a journal with you everywhere for a week or two just to remind yourself that you are surrounded by writing prompts. You may need to slowly work your way into practicing the Examen by starting with just a few questions.

Perhaps you need to keep your expectations really, really low at first.

What if you told yourself that it's enough to be still and present, trusting that God is with you in this moment?

What if you told yourself that writing will happen soon enough if you can stop yourself and focus on a single idea?

Then you can build from there.

You may end up praying in ways you didn't expect. You may end up writing about something completely different than what you'd planned.

In fact, you may end up writing and praying about the very things you've most wanted to forget. That's no accident. Writing and prayer can actually become avenues of inner healing and personal growth. As you cultivate these practices, your writing and prayer can also become sources of healing and personal growth for others as well.

CHAPTER THREE

DO YOU WANT TO BE MADE WELL?

Are We Hiding or Healing Our Pain?
When I look back at my childhood, there are two important moments that speak volumes to how I've dealt with pain in my life. The first is a quiet morning during my childhood where I sat by myself completely absorbed in a hockey video game. In the other, I was a teenager sitting on my bed listening to punk rock. Both moments could be innocent, everyday experiences for the average child or teenager, however, there was so much more going on beneath the surface.

I've been anxious and worried for most of my life, and I can trace the origin of those traits back to my parents' divorce and combative relationship. Almost every memory of my early childhood involves my parents screaming at each other. I found a lot of safety during my early years at my grandparents' home, where I lived with my mom until my teen years. While I played hockey, stickball, and football outside with my friends every week, I also spent hours playing video games in their den. While my mom was determined to make me go outside and play, I craved the peace and order of a video game where I just had to worry about following the rules in the game and could immerse myself in an alternate reality.

I gave up on video games in high school when I took a deeper interest in the punk rock bands that had been making the rounds at my high school. I would lie in bed with anger and resentment burning against my parents and all of the kids in my high school who were cruel to me, and it would come to a full raging boil as the singers shouted and wailed. Without passing judgment on anyone's preferences for how they spend their free time or their taste in music, video games and music became my escapes from the pain of my life. While entertainment can provide a healthy escape as we unwind after a busy day, it's a terrible strategy for dealing with pain and the difficulties of life.

I recognize that some people have experienced so many things that were far worse than what I went through in my childhood. I had a lot of stable relationships, never suffered abuse, and always had support from my parents and grandparents. However, the fear and anxiety of those early years were very real and powerful. They can haunt me today when I find myself struggling with anxiety for no reason in particular. Anxiety and fear became habits that have worn their way into my life after years of practice. I also suspect they are behind my desire to control my life circumstances and the rage I feel when circumstances don't line up the way I want. So many events in my early life felt completely chaotic and out of control, that I've made myself a nervous, controlling wreck trying to reassert control over at least a few things.

When I look back at all of the time I spent trying to distract myself and exert control over my life with video games and music, I can see in retrospect that I was trying to either avoid the difficult parts of my life or to feed the anger that I felt growing inside of myself with angry music. Either way, I wasn't actually dealing with the pain and reaching a point of forgiveness or resolution. One of the most important steps I took toward becoming a healthy person was removing both punk rock and video games completely from my life for a season. I'm not saying this is the right thing for everyone. Rather, at that point in my life I needed to cut myself off from the music that had been feeding my anger and the video games that shut my mind off from the pain of my past. I needed to feel my pain and confront it.

Here's the thing about the pain of our pasts, we can't really escape it no matter how many defenses we adopt or how far we run. We can't completely ignore it. It has a way of unsettling us and showing up at the most inconvenient times. I face the fall out of my anxiety and anger every single day whether or not I act like it doesn't exist. It's far better to acknowledge that we've been worn down and wounded so that we can forgive others and begin to heal.

In one of the stories where Jesus healed a paralyzed man, he asked the man a fascinating question: "Do you want to be made well?" We would think that this question hardly needs to be asked, but we quickly learn that the man had bought into a local legend about the healing power of a nearby pool of water as a way of explaining away his pain. He was so absorbed in muddling along as things were that he couldn't see an opportunity to be set free.

As we pray, we have an opportunity to open our deepest wounds to God in order to receive healing. However, if we want to be healed, we have to move beyond merely believing in God's power to heal. We have to actually open ourselves up to God. I have personally found that saying something out loud can help. If I can hear myself saying that I was fearful, angry, and worried all of the time as a child and teenager, I can no longer deny it. That means I'm digging up all of that pain and fear all over again, and it's pretty much the worst thing ever. This is all of the stuff I want to forget and bury. Nevertheless, each day I spend struggling with anxiety and fear is a reminder that I haven't fully dealt with these issues from my past. God has brought healing to these areas of my life, but only when I have been fully honest and open about the extent of the pain when I've prayed. In fact, some of my most profound experiences in prayer have been directly related to voicing the pain of my past.

We don't just heal by articulating past pain when we pray. We can also heal by writing about our pain, our fears, and our struggles. As my prayer and writing work together, I have often transitioned from prayer to writing as I've faced the anxiety of my past. I've found tremendous healing and perspective by writing about my current struggles with anxiety, anger, and control. By stepping back from the day to day events that seem to spiral out of control and seem to inevitably lead to anger, writing has provided an invaluable bird's eye perspective.

While there is always a possibility of writers over-sharing at times, our most authentic and powerful writing will almost always come from facing the pain of our past. That doesn't mean we have to share all of the details with the public. We have to define our own limits here. However, if we write about the things have been formative, important, or emotionally powerful for us, we'll be extremely motivated to write because we'll have a sense of urgency about the topics. We'll also be far more inclined to write in our own voice since we're writing out of something intensely personal and real to us. There will be less temptation to write in a particular way that we imagine "professional" authors should write about such things. Most importantly, writing provides a way to process and think deeply about difficult topics. Some find writing to be more beneficial for sorting out their thoughts than others, but almost every writer I know finds great value in taking time to articulate their thoughts on the page or screen. Much like voicing our pain verbally while praying, there is a tremendous amount of power that comes from honestly writing out the truth of our pain and struggles.

Having said all of that, our culture provides every tool we could ever need to avoid facing our pain, praying about it, or writing about it at length. The noise and pace of modern life can fast become ways to medicate ourselves from our past or present pain, but so can drugs, alcohol, sex, and entertainment. There's a new app every week that provides yet another way to escape the most difficult parts of our lives. Distraction is the key to many technology business plans these days, providing apps, games, and information that will prevent us from taking time for self-reflection--the very practice that could expose the most difficult parts of our lives. As such, we'll struggle to find the healing and peace we need so badly.

Writing and prayer aren't just fun activities or amusements. They're critical lifelines as we strive to become healthy, whole people in our communities. They'll help us shine a light on the darkest moments from the past so that we can be healed and reach a place of greater clarity.

Vulnerability Prompts Writing and Prayer

Perhaps it's most difficult to begin writing because we're hesitant to address the topics that we most need to confront. The pain we carry and the vulnerable parts of our lives often need to be front and center for both prayer and writing (with some important caveats to follow!) because they will prompt us to be our most honest and authentic. Our wounds are too real and the pain too great to hide. These may be personal failures, disappointments, secrets, or wounds that we've received from others.

If you made a list of bestselling books, whether fiction or nonfiction, it's likely that the majority explore brokenness, pain, and conflict. It's no mystery that most stories and poems deal with either death or love, and the latter can often involve quite a bit of conflict as characters fall in love or out of love. As books grapple with life and death, love and loss, we confront problems and failures.

In fact, we wouldn't want to read a book about a perfect character who never struggles with character flaws, a difficult past, or interpersonal conflict. Writers can powerfully connect with readers when they venture to these thin places of pain and brokenness because readers can see themselves in the pain and want to journey from pain and struggle toward redemption or some kind of resolution.

That isn't to say that our writing must always confront the worst parts of our past. I'm also not saying we have to write about every single detail in order to be vulnerable. While complete honesty is important for prayer, writing for an audience will call for discernment about what needs to be said, what can be excluded, and which details can be altered for the sake of personal privacy.

This a step in our growth as writers and people of faith who are grounded and aware of ourselves, able to see both the hard parts of life and the hope we have for healing in the future. We will also have to face our pain time and time again as new challenges and tragedies arise, but this may only be one aspect of your writing. However, you shouldn't be surprised if readers tell you that your best writing addresses your deepest struggles. Likewise, you shouldn't be surprised that your most significant moments in prayer come when you face the difficult aspects of your past.

If you can't be fully honest to God in prayer, I'd suggest prayer will only be an exercise in futility. It's not a stretch to suggest that God probably has a *pretty good idea* of what you've done or failed to do, right? In fact, the most tragic lament of God throughout the Bible is that God's people have not brought their pain and failures to be healed. If they could just turn back to God, they could be healed. The stories about Jesus show him setting the bar quite low for healing people. When a father confessed that he needed help with his "unbelief," Jesus still healed his son.

If you can't bring yourself to be honest in your writing, then you have to ask whether you're projecting a false self for readers. Are you writing in your own voice? Are you afraid you won't be able to find your own voice? Are you afraid of confronting your pain, fears, and failures in black and white on the page? While spelling these things out in writing will help, there's a good reason why I'm linking writing and prayer together. Writing can only offer us so much by way of healing. The writing process may unearth pain or past wounds that we simply can't handle on our own. Sometimes we can only find healing and hope through prayer.

For those who feel stuck in either writing or prayer, this is one way to move forward: if you want to grow in prayer and writing, you have to dig into your deepest pain and struggles. The faster you confront your shame, failures, and past wounds, the faster you'll find God and the faster you'll write something that could be truly meaningful.

This, however, is extremely risky.

What if you dig up the pain of the past and you don't experience God?

What if you write about the deepest hurts in your life and no one cares?

I've been there, and I've struggled through the process. Sometimes progress feels really, really slow. Nevertheless, these are the kinds of difficult questions that every writer or person of faith faces at one time or another. They are part of the leap of faith we must take in order to pray and write with freedom and health. They also lead us to an important consideration about our motivations.

Why We Write and Pray

I trust that you're drawn to both prayer and writing because there's something inside of you that keeps pushing you to take another step forward. In fact, you may also have someone or something prompting you from the outside as well. Perhaps a friend has encouraged you to dig deeper into writing or prayer through either personal example or a few encouraging words.

While every writer craves to be read, and those who pray crave for God to respond, we have to step out in faith without knowing where our actions will lead us. In fact, I can't tell you where any of this will lead you. I can only speak of generalities and trends. This is why it can be immensely helpful to have a friend or group to support you through either endeavor. In fact, you will most likely struggle with prayer and writing if you pursue either in isolation. Some of my most important steps forward in prayer and writing occurred because someone challenged me or guided the way forward.

We will begin to see growth in prayer and writing by committing to the process. It will take time. There will be struggles. We will have to send out S.O.S. signals at times. They may be frequent if we actually face the pain that is simmering below the surface in our lives.

Writing and Praying about Pain

One of my friends is a popular and prolific blogger. She gets paid quite well to write sponsored blog posts, to blog about traveling around the world, or to just post an Instagram wearing a piece of jewelry. She's invited to speak at conferences and has editors dropping book deals into her lap. While she has written plenty of excellent posts that I've read, there's one short post that stands out for me. She wrote a short piece as part of a link up with other bloggers about being vulnerable. It was like reading about myself. Despite her accomplishments and popularity, she worried about people liking her, she obsessed over how she presented herself to others, and she got stressed about the future just like me. Besides standing out in my mind as the best post she's ever written, that post also helped me see her writing with new eyes. Here is someone coming from the same exact place as myself.

Around the same time that I read my friend's blog post (and most likely inspired by her), I began to reflect on my own insecurities and failures. There were several moments from my teen and young adult years that have hounded me, especially the moments when I'd betrayed friends or had been ridiculously selfish. They were like scenes in a movie that, once recalled, replayed themselves in my mind in an endless, cringe-worthy loop that made me feel like dirt. My moments of greatest failure had been hounding me and pumping a steady stream of anxiety and discouragement into my life. I hardly felt worthy of God, let alone of my family and friends.

When you're hounded by the shame of the past, you can turn into a pretty miserable person who is always trying to measure up

46

and please others. You're always gauging the responses of others and obsessing over the most minor gesture or response.

One afternoon I sat down to pray because I'd had enough of the shame I'd been carrying. While I don't always have profound experiences with God when I sit down to pray, this moment of surrender brought God's presence like a great big "WHOOSH!" It was like a private Pentecost. I sensed God's Spirit dwelling with me and comforting me. I saw that confessing my shame became a kind of highway that helped me immediately connect with God.

I brought the stuff to God that I felt like I needed to hide, even if it sounds foolish to think I could ever hide anything from God. God had been willing to heal me all along, but I first needed to extend an invitation through honesty. My greatest leaps forward in both prayer and writing required unflinching confession about my greatest pain and failures.

By the same token, some of my most powerful writing has come from my sources of pain and shame. And to a certain degree, this makes perfect sense.

I can't think of many people who want to read about all of the ways I'm an awesome father. However, if I write about the times I lose my temper with my kids or the ways I'm dealing with my frustration at my kid's tantrums, people will immediately recognize themselves. I can also share my process and the steps that have been healing as I confront my anger--this need not be all doom and gloom. By confessing my shortfalls as a parent, I'm once again creating a point of connection with others. Time and time again, I've seen writers and fellow believers make meaningful connections with others in the dark valleys of pain and shame.

If no one is reading what you write or prayer feels like you're just talking in an empty room, there's a chance that you need to dig into your pain, shame, and failure. You need to look at your struggles and decide what you can write about.

For instance, every writer I know talks about Anne Lamott's book *Bird by Bird* because she perfectly captures the envy that writers have for each other. This is a dark, ugly secret that many of us carry around, but Lamott bravely tackles it and now every writer I know talks about her book--that part in particular. As she talks about fighting off her envy, we're able to relate because we've connected with her through her shame and weakness. In fact, now that I've related with Lamott at her lowest point, I'm also able to relate to her moments of triumph.

This idea of relating to others through pain and suffering runs throughout the Bible. Jesus came down to earth in order to bear our burdens alongside us so that he could, in part, empathize with us. Through Jesus' ministry and death, God entered into our pain alongside us. Rather than removing the mysteries of pain, suffering, and evil, the Bible reveals a God who meets us where we suffer the most. It's no surprise that our prayer lives will flourish when we join ourselves with God through our pain.

Restoring Others through Prayer and Writing

My in-laws have been ministering in prisons among some of the most broken men I've ever met. Before these men broke the law and wounded others, they were often neglected, abused, and violated by friends, family, and strangers. Their journey of healing is intense and fraught with challenges. When I've gone into the prison to talk with these men and pray with them, I've found that I can best minister to them by sharing the ways God has healed my own pain.

In other words, I can pass on what God has done in me. Ministry, especially prayer ministry, is all about becoming whole and healthy so that we can pass along God's restoration to others. My in-laws say, "First God does it to you, then he does it through you." There's a reason why the early church passed along the Holy Spirit by laying hands on each other.

While God wants to heal and restore us, the healing we receive isn't just for us. We don't just pursue prayer in order to make ourselves better. Our healing may not be fully complete until we've passed it along to others.

We will also grow as writers when we see our work as an act of service to others. Of course we hope to sell enough copies of our books to make our work sustainable, but we will always be discouraged and dissatisfied if we're looking at our website views or sales numbers for fulfillment. There will always be someone who grows a bigger blog, sells more copies, gets better reviews, or lands a better publishing deal.

If you want to define yourself as a successful writer, aim to help others. If you can help someone, then you're a success. Share your low points and how you've battled through them. Share your biggest doubts, challenges, and failures so that readers can join you in your journey. Write about the thing you fear the most. We can, in part, redeem the low points and valleys of our lives by inviting others into our journeys.

The way to healing is always through our pain because pain connects us with God. Pain also breaks through the false identities we create as writers. Our pain doesn't have to get the last word. In fact, we can defeat pain by using it as a jumping off point for our healing and restoration. We can defeat pain by helping others overcome the pain they face in their own lives.

Until we face that pain, we'll be left wondering what's getting in the way of our relationships with God and what's missing from our creative process.

CHAPTER FOUR

BREAKING THROUGH WITH SELF-AWARENESS

How Our Bodies Warn Us

Writing and prayer are both physical activities, even if they usually involve minimal motion. Prayer is often a posture communicating reverence and a commitment to be present as much as it's a two-way conversation. Physically speaking, writing can be little more than scratching a pen across a page or typing on a keyboard, but one's body is still very much involved in the writing process. We can slouch when exhausted, hunch over the screen when working on a problem, or sit grinding our teeth together when a project isn't quite coming together.

Awareness of our bodies can lead us to significant breakthroughs in both writing and prayer. Far too much has been made of struggling to focus the mind for prayer or keeping the mind fresh to write when our bodies are screaming many of the most important things we need to know. In fact, our bodies may tell us whether we're about to have a frustrating writing session, what kind of writing we should pursue, and even what we should pray about.

Having said that, we also need to know what's going on in our minds. Our bodies act a bit like an early warning alarm that can give us clues about what's going on in our minds, but without regular time to take stock of our physical and mental states, we'll struggle to write and pray.

Oftentimes we have significant issues bubbling beneath the surfaces of our minds. Many are afraid to look long enough to truly see them. Fear, anxiety, self-doubt, or anger can all derail us in our writing and prayer. If we don't develop some simple self-awareness practices, many of our greatest weaknesses will continue to hold us back.

The Keys to Physical Awareness

Did you know that your body gives clues about your mental and spiritual states? This has been a basic starting point for the physical therapy that has made the biggest difference for me. I've gone to physical therapy for neck and shoulder strain that have resulted from a combination of my writing work. I didn't expect our sessions to also address my psychological pain associated with anxiety. The sources of pain in my body could be traced right back to my mind, but my body offered up all of the most important clues.

I've learned to recognize the following signs of stress or anxiety:

- Clenched teeth.
- Balled up fists.
- Shortness of breath.
- Arched shoulders.
- A stiff or craned neck.
- Feet crunched up in a starting block position.

I've also cracked the soles of three pairs of shoes from bending them in a crunched up, starting block position. I use the starting block connection with running on purpose.

When I first attended a physical therapy session, the therapist said that my body was in a constant "fight or flight" state, as if I was keeping alert for a tiger attack. While this was insightful and helpful, I also couldn't help thinking, "Well yeah, terrible things could happen at any moment!"

Fear and anxiety had become my baseline for normal life. I didn't even know it was possible to live without almost literally crippling anxiety. Living responsibly meant living in constant fear of something terrible happening. For instance, I always expected my boss at work to call with bad news, a client to email a complaint, or an editor to write with the worst news imaginable. Of course all of that has happened at one point or another in the past. Armed with my limited anecdotal evidence, I began to live in a constant state of anxiety, anticipating the worst at any moment. In fact, there have been plenty of times when I don't even know what I'm worried about. I'm just worried in general.

I received a lot of prayer for my struggles with anxiety and fear that brought change and freedom, but second to receiving prayer, the most important step for me was learning to recognize the signs of anxiety in my body. When did my breathing grow difficult? When did I clench my teeth? When did I arch my shoulders up or lean over my computer while writing?

I started to pinpoint the parts of my life that were controlled by fear, and that helped me pray in the midst of specific struggles. I also started to uncover some of the obstacles standing in the way of my writing. For instance, certain projects that were extremely important to me always resulted in a stiff neck from hunching over the computer. Lingering below the surface was a baseline of anxiety that expected the worst to happen with my writing.

My best work always comes from the times when I'm completely immersed in a project and don't have to constantly battle self-doubts and fear. However, I had the most anxiety in the midst of the work that meant the most to me. If I already have a baseline of anxiety, then it's particularly challenging to hit a point of creative freedom where I can fully give myself to my work. Mind you, I can get there eventually, and it certainly helps to be aware of what's going on in my body and mind, but it takes a lot of intentional work to sit up straight, to relax my shoulders, to slow my breathing with deep breaths, and to give my mind freedom to completely focus on the project at hand.

In the same way, there are physical strategies for finding greater freedom while praying. My physical therapist suggested practices such as tensing up my feet and releasing the tension, as well as balling up a fist and then releasing it into an open hand. Lifting some light weights, stretching, or using exercise bands have all helped as well. In addition to these exercises, I can approach prayer with a similar mindset of releasing tension: I leave my hands palms up and open--the exact opposite of my clenched fists that signal fear and control issues.

While we don't automatically pray by opening our hands "palms up," we are taking an intentionally open and welcoming stance toward God. We are letting go of our worries and fears in order to receive the comfort and healing God offers. We're also prepared to offer these gifts to others.

Perhaps you can explore other postures for prayer that communicate resting or complete trust in God. I have sometimes dropped to my knees next to my couch in a moment of surrender or trust in God for a particular situation. Sometimes holding a prayer book will help you focus. Others have found the structure of Rosary beads comforting since they offer a place to concentrate nervous energy while reciting prayers.

However you feel comfortable dealing with physical manifestations of pain, fear, or anxiety in your prayer and writing, there's another step that will lead to even greater freedom. After addressing the physical symptoms, we can take action that addresses the sources of our pain and struggles.

Praying and Writing with the Examen
There are many practices in the Christian tradition that can help

us take steps forward in personal awareness for both prayer and writing, but I have found the Examen among the most helpful in this season of my life. It has proven invaluable for guiding my prayer life and providing no end of writing prompts.

I began practicing the Examen after a friend recommended an app called "Examine," which guides users through a series of practices and questions. I found it at a time when I was learning to be self-aware, but I struggled to know how to process the stress, discouragement, and anxiety I'd been uncovering. The Examen app I used asked questions such as: What keeps you awake at night? What discouraged you today?

For instance, money has been a constant source of stress since I started freelancing full time. A combination of unfortunate circumstances and failed plans on my part put us in the hole after my first year as a freelancer, and a series of up and down months persisted for a few years until I established a solid client base. Even if my writing work has moved to a place of greater stability, the Examen revealed that the habit of worrying about money from those early years stuck. That was just the beginning of the revelations about my work.

I also frequently reported that I was discouraged or just a little encouraged, and my reasons were often tied to my writing work. I wanted my influential friends to like my work and to champion me in the same way they championed each other. If I had a little more influence and visibility, I reasoned that I could make more money so that we wouldn't have to worry about running out of our cash reserves. I wanted to move our family to a greater place of stability, and I measured my progress with the smallest of metrics each day, such as a tweet sharing my work. Needless to say, I wasn't in a healthy place!

As I put so much stock in those desires to succeed at writing, I also began to measure the good parts of my day according to the success of my writing work. If I landed a new client, made progress on a project, or received a decent-sized check, I could mark up that day as an encouraging success. However, there were many other times when I couldn't let myself relax because I hadn't made enough progress that day. While there's nothing wrong with celebrating success at work, I began to let my day hinge on what happened at work.

I hadn't looked at my marriage, children, or friendships as sources of encouragement or goodness. In my drive to be a provider for my family, I had turned my work into an idol and a measuring stick for my self-worth. The Examen helped me spot these misplaced priorities and prompted me to change how I spent my day and how I measured the positive and negative aspects of my day.

I started to celebrate the simple moments when I could sit with our toddler before bed and recount the day. I started to thank God for the chats my wife and I had while I washed the dishes. I saw the value in our infant's joyful smiles when we locked eyes with him. I also prioritized walks with the kids and getting home on time for dinner rather than pushing to finish one... more... thing. I shut my computer down after completing my work so that I wouldn't be tempted to open it one more time in the evening. After a few months of shifting my perspective and practices while praying, I noticed that my anxiety had dropped, and I was still getting just as much work done--if not more.

You don't have to practice the Examen in order to benefit from the basic concept. It's basically just a tool for self-reflection. Our greatest mistake in life is that we can keep pushing ourselves to move faster from one thing to another. If we aren't making progress, we can make the mistake of trying to work harder, faster, or with greater organization. Sometimes we just need to stop and take stock of ourselves and the people around us before moving on to the next project, before we add one more "tool" that will make everything better, or before we take a course that promises epic organization and productivity.

Spiritual and Mental Maintenance

Pastor John Wesley, one of the most influential figures in the

First Great Awakening and founder of the Methodist denomination, routinely started small group meetings with a series of questions that helped each person discern the state of his or her soul. The early Methodist question, "How is it with your soul?" could be updated to: How is your soul doing?

This is a bit deeper than, "How are you doing?" This question asks us to look at how our spiritual, emotional, and mental states are developing, conflicting, or thriving. We are called to look at the ways our outer actions flow from an inner spiritual state.

At the risk of sounding too mechanical, this is a basic act of personal "maintenance." We're looking at the ways we're either functioning well or breaking down and then looking at the spiritual factors behind either. Even if we're doing well, we shouldn't assume that we'll continue running in top form without regular breaks. If we're struggling, we can take heart that there is hope for us.

This chapter, and really this whole book, is all about simple steps we can take to improve our spiritual, physical, and mental states as we seek to pray and write. If you're struggling with writing or prayer, Wesley's question is a good place to begin. A little self-reflection will help you tap into what you may need to write or pray about. Then again, you may feel a need to either unplug yourself when possible or take some time to rest.

We need both short and long-term rest. While I find that I always need to write something no matter how weary or refreshed I am, the kind of writing I do will change depending on the season of life. A big push to finish a book may be followed by a week or two of lighter journaling and straightforward writing for a few clients. And while I routinely pray the hours and practice the Examen each week, I sometimes need a long stretch of devotional reading or a bit of time immersed in Bible reading.

Several friends have benefitted from giving up social media completely for Lent, while others have put firm boundaries around social media, such as logging off for the weekend or removing the related apps from their smart phones. They didn't make these choices just to be trendy or self-righteous. They spent time in self-examination and realized their souls could use a break. If you haven't spent significant time, at least 24 hours, away from social media or your smart phone, then it's certainly time to give it a shot. You may try abstaining from social media for all of Sunday. Then again, I have found that removing Facebook from my tablet is often enough to keep myself off social media on nights and weekends.

On the weekends I always make a point of reading for a sustained period of time in the afternoon without "social media breaks." In the warmer months I find tremendous restoration out in the garden, even if it's just pulling out a bunch of dead plants in the fall. In fact, I have found tremendous peace from restoring order and simplicity to the garden after a productive season. Others have found tremendous benefit in running or walking regularly, noting that exercise provides both stress relief and time to pray or simply gather their thoughts.

Whether you use exercise or the Examen as a way to make a daily check in, we'll all break down without some regular maintenance. If we don't stop to ask the tough questions on our own, we will most certainly break down in the future and the restoration process will be far more complicated and involved at that point.

Continually binging on entertainment, food, or work can all negatively impact our souls and our relationships. We'll also leave little time for spiritual growth or creative pursuits. However, if we don't stop long enough to reflect on tough questions or to notice the signs our bodies are sending us, we'll start to wonder what's wrong when we can't focus on an important writing project or our minds begin racing when we try to pray. Time for maintenance often means abstaining from certain practices in order to find out what life is like without them. If we notice that our lives tilt too far toward chaos, anxiety, or lack of focus, perhaps we've let entertainment take up too much space. A maintenance check allows us to restore a healthy balance through boundaries or regular periods of fasting from entertainment.

Maintenance can be difficult and inconvenient. Sometimes maintenance reveals problems that can only be resolved by making big changes in how we live. By developing personal awareness, we're able to see our problems and obstacles with refreshing clarity. In fact, we'll be best prepared to orient ourselves outward, seeing the needs of others and serving them, if we first turn in to ourselves and invite God to bring healing. If we can break down the barriers that keep us from God, from each other, and from our creative pursuits, we'll be able to pray, write, or relate with greater freedom. When we've found better clarity, restored balance to our lives, and experienced healing, we'll be in a much healthier place to think of how our writing and prayer can serve others.

Rather than acting from a place of fear, anxiety, distraction, or anger, we'll be able to share the healing and restoration that has come from our prayer and writing. In fact, we'll finally be able to tap into our passions, which will lead to some truly wonderful gifts we can share.

CHAPTER FIVE

DISCERNMENT THROUGH PRAYER AND WRITING

Finding the Path Forward

I've spent far too many years worrying about what I'd do with my life or how I'd ever earn a sustainable income. I couldn't think of a single skill or talent that I had since I believed "writer" is right up there with "professional candy taster" or "video game tester" in the unrealistic career column.

People kept telling me to become a doctor or lawyer, but I find hospital stuff gross and legal stuff bores me no end. I'm more of a "close enough" kind of guy--the worst person for either profession. The same went for not following in my dad's footsteps as a plumber. Solder shmoder... as long as the pipes kind of fit together I figured we could call it a day and pick up a water ice on the way home.

Of course I had gifts, passions, and talents, but they were creative in nature. I had ruled out writing so completely that I didn't even know you could work as a copywriter. This was before the television show Mad Men introduced me to that world. On second thought, that's probably all for the best any way.

I didn't start writing as a career just because I loved it. While I love writing, I started writing because I felt like I was literally out of options in my mid-twenties. The more I invested in writing and practiced prayer, the more I saw how they worked together to direct and refine my passions and calling in life. Whether or not you plan to write professionally, writing and prayer are powerful tools for sorting out the direction of your life. As it turns out, the more I wrote and prayed, the more I felt compelled to keep writing and to keep praying. I trust that every reader of this book will have different passions, interests, and directions for their lives. The common denominator is that writing and prayer are essential discernment tools, especially when we face big, life-altering decisions.

However, before we get into the ways writing and prayer can function as tools for discernment, we need a rather large caveat before we talk about the ways writing and prayer can direct our passions and life choices. The caveat: One's passion may not be the same as one's day job.

Sometimes we have to do the work that we need to do in order to pay the bills--period. While writing and prayer can provide direction for our lives, I also don't want to put anyone's financial future in jeopardy. While writing can pay the bills for a few of us, I'm more interested in encouraging you to find the ways writing can help us grow personally and spiritually.

There are some who have found the perfect mix of work and passion. Maybe others need to just be really pragmatic about their work for a season. And then perhaps some prefer to keep their passions separate from their day (or night) jobs. I mainly want to make it clear that writing and prayer can help direct and fulfill your passions even if your day job isn't tied directly to them.

Once we've ironed out a plan for financial survival, we can talk a bit more about our passions and what it would look like to make them part of our prayer and writing. There's nothing wrong with pursuing a passion, especially a God-given passion as part of your work, but it may not always be a full time career that pays the bills.

We can't always find the perfect job or career that fits our precise talents, personal priorities, or spiritual calling. Some have arrived there and some are working on getting there, but if we're seeking the most perfect match to our passions in our work, we may never be satisfied. Or we may just go broke, which I don't think anyone is passionate about. In fact, by seeking fulfillment in a particular kind of job, we may end up making work into an idol that we serve in order to reach fulfillment.

Having said all of that, you may find that your writing will thrive the most when you tap into your passions and deepest desires. At the very least, writing about major decisions, mundane issues, and important challenges will help you figure out what you care about the most and may help you make work, family, or leisure decisions that vastly improve your quality of life.

In the same way, prayer helps us cut through the dead ends, imbalances, and unhealthy practices of our lives. In prayer we are free to see what matters most and can discern where God is leading us. In fact, we may find that our supposed passions have been misplaced. We may find peace and contentment through new passions that are realigned by God's influence in our lives. In fact, those are the "passions" that are worth pursuing.

When I talk about pursuing a "calling" or a "passion" here, I'm specifically addressing a God-given drive or desire. Sometimes a passion has to be discovered and cultivated. More times than not, our experiences direct us toward certain causes or objectives, and practices such as prayer and writing help us work toward greater clarity and balance as we determine the way forward.

Discovering Our Passions

We've spent a lot of time looking at the ways that writing and prayer can help us deal with the negative aspects of our lives, but once we've sorted out some of these obstacles, we're in a better position to move forward with our passions in positive directions.

Most importantly, people of faith should begin with prayer because we're not so much concerned with "our" passions per se. This is where my own Christian tradition comes into particularly sharp focus. The Christian faith teaches that God is fully capable of speaking to us if we can learn to listen.

Part of our growth in prayer involves reorienting our desires in healthy directions--directions that are guided by the Holy Spirit for our own benefit and the benefit of others. So as we talk about our passions, it's actually the passions that God has shaped within us. Our experiences and gifts certainly play into the development of these passions, but ultimately it's God's influence that orients us in healthy directions that enables us to pursue them in healthy and loving ways.

As you pray and write each day, start asking yourself what really stirs your emotions.

What are the things that you can't stop yourself from thinking about?

Are there things in your day-to-day life that you keep noticing over and over and over again?

Are there people you especially admire and even envy a little because of the work they do?

Who are you drawn to pray about?

In what ways are your drawn to help others?

What are you consistently grateful for?

What gives you anxiety attacks?

What leaves you fulfilled and grateful as you offer thanks to God?

These are the things to start praying about more specifically.

Once you've learned how to notice the negative aspects of your life, you'll also learn how to recognize the positive aspects that drive your passions. In fact, without the negative distractions of anxiety or fear, you'll be prepared to see the good things around you that offer life and affirmation. Without the noise of negativity and fear, you'll begin to discern God's still, small voice.

As we learn to hear God's voice and recognize what stirs our spirits, we'll be guided in more fulfilling directions for prayer and writing. We'll begin to tap into the burdens that God has placed on us, and our writing will begin to resonate with topics and stories that touch something within us.

By embracing these passions in prayer and writing, we'll find that our connections with others will be deeper as well. Mind you, if you publish about these topics, that doesn't mean you'll find a huge readership or fame and fortune. You may still have a small group of readers, but they will respond to the authenticity of your writing. Best yet, as you move into your passions through self-reflection and prayer, you'll have words of life and encouragement to share.

While we're all drawn to people who are passionate, that doesn't mean people are always drawn to healthy, life-giving passions. In fact, more often than not, readers, especially online, are drawn to people who are passionate about fighting perceived threats and attacking those who are different. Those who are passionate about attacking and dismantling something may have good reasons for their work, but such passionate conflict must eventually give way to redemption.

It's no mistake that readers are drawn to conflict. Conflict is the driving force of novels and nonfiction narratives. However, conflict can become an addicting toxin in our writing if we rely on it to connect with readers. At a certain point we will burn out and so will many of our readers. Unfortunately, conflict may draw in enough new readers that this lack of retention won't matter.

While there are some instances where conflict with an idea or personality is called for, our greater goal in writing and prayer is to become healthy people who can serve others. Facing our inner conflicts can prompt deeper life change as we pray and produce writing that is more beneficial and also make us healthier members of our communities. We'll certainly grow by practicing prayer and writing in community, but we have to choose to make the first step to boldly face the conflicts in our lives through prayer and writing. As we heal, we'll find at least part of our passions. Our passions may even end up being the very things we'd rather avoid in prayer and writing.

For instance, my parents' divorce and my difficult history with the church have both developed my passions to write about parenting and healing from church conflict. Through a combination of prayer and journaling, I've found a deeper sense of calling to write about these topics. I would say that I have a "passion" to write about both, and writing about them has proven extremely fulfilling.

Mind you, I'm rarely ever paid to write about either of these topics, at least as of this writing. I blog for businesses and write or edit eBooks to help pay the bills. I write and edit because they're things I can do to earn a living wage within my skill set, but in my free time I write about prayer, writing, and parenting because I'm passionate about them. I wouldn't complain if I ended up finding a more sustainable career that ties into my particular passions, but the pursuit of our passions shouldn't hinge on finding a 40-hour a week job that enables us to immerse ourselves in them.

Cultivating Our Passions

Tapping into our passions can feel optional after we've accomplished our work, fed our families, done the dishes, put the kids to bed, and picked up the house. Who doesn't want to plop on the couch and switch to autopilot as the television magically delivers enchantment and wonder after a hard day?

I feel that pull too, and it's not an entirely bad thing. Sometimes we need to switch into autopilot and decompress a bit. But the kind of entertainment offered by television is more like an enjoyable candy to be consumed in moderation rather than a four-hour binge of a make-believe world that promises the fulfillment of a "meal." What if you made it a rule that you at least have to match every minute of entertainment with focused time spent in writing and/or prayer? If we don't make sacrifices to write and pray, we'll never tap into our passions.

Even if you dedicated part of that focused time to reading a book on writing or spirituality, you'll at least be inspired to keep working at both disciplines. That is the hard part of this book's message. Writing and prayer will most certainly feel like work at the start and require a certain amount of intentionality and persistence in order to keep up with them. As time goes by, you'll develop strengths and begin to see growth as prayer and writing become habits. Better yet, the work of writing and the discipline of prayer will start to bring rewards on their own. It won't always be a struggle to focus or to fill a page with words. It won't always feel like a huge sacrifice to switch off the television to pray or write. You'll begin to recognize a need to do both.

Before you move on in this book, take a moment to reflect on what it would look like to intentionally cultivate the practices of prayer and writing in your life. Perhaps they'll look different on weekdays rather than weekends, so you can set different goals depending on each.

Starting out is always the most difficult stage. Gardeners know that the work of spring is often the most taxing part of the season. You have to dig up the soil to work in compost, leaves, and other fertilizers in order to create a healthy growing environment. After you've turned over the soil and planned your plots, you'll have to build a trellis for hanging beans or set up cages for the tomatoes. You'll have to put up a fence to keep squirrels and rabbits out. You'll have to thin out your new seedlings and carefully manage how much water they receive.

However, if you invest in a healthy gardening environment in the spring, you'll reap tremendous benefits by summer time. Besides having food to eat, you'll only have to do some watering and weeding when needed.

I believe that every person has a lot of potential for life and health through the disciplines of writing and prayer. We all have our own obstacles and challenges to overcome, but we all share the same potential for health and an abundant harvest. However, the first step toward an abundant harvest is digging into the most barren parts of our lives and turning things upside down.

Sharing Our Passions with Others

I don't want this book to be merely about personal improvement. While we begin with sorting out our mental and spiritual health and personally connecting with God at times, this is a process where progress is best made in community. In fact, it's often the help of a trusted friend that will make the difference. In addition, our end goal in all of this is service to others.

I'm reminded of a story from the Gospels where Jesus spent an entire evening praying on a mountain. We don't know what he said or if he even said anything at all to God. We can only presume that he needed this time before selecting his disciples on the following day.

While the disciples traveled with Jesus and ministered alongside him, there's no doubt that he spent a tremendous amount of time investing in them individually. They also received significant benefits from the time Jesus spent away from them in prayer.

If we want to share something meaningful and healing with others, we have to spend time up on the mountain. We have to break away from our "important" goals and projects. We have to silence the noise around us and turn away from the urgent problems fighting to capture our attention. While we can't completely disconnect from the responsibilities and challenges of life, we have to create time and space where our writing and prayer can develop and thrive.

As we invest in them, we'll have more to offer others. And if working on both disciplines at once strikes you as too much right now, just try focusing on one. Besides, developing your writing will help you pray and learning to pray will help you write. The two are connected. You may grow in ways that will surprise you. You may share things with others that change their lives.

That last point is really what it's all about, whether that "it" is praying or writing. We pray, write, and grow because we were made to experience abundant life and to share that abundant life with others. If we try to bottle it up for ourselves, we'll miss out on the greatest joys of prayer and creativity. We all have something to offer others. I have yet to meet a single person who doesn't have something valuable and unique to offer. However, too many people fail to realize what that is. As a result they suffer from a sense of diminished self worth and feel like they can't help anyone.

Writing and prayer, especially when practiced together, can help break that stalemate. Writing and prayer can help you discover what's been holding you back so that you can begin to grow. When you begin to grow, you'll have something to offer others, and that changes everything. With these goals in mind, you'll be in a better position to take the leap of faith that writing and prayer require.

CHAPTER SIX

WE PRAY AND WRITE BY FAITH

The Leap into Writing and Prayer

Writing and prayer are both leaps into the dark.

We have faith that words and God are there to be found if we seek them with all of our hearts.

Mastering the disciplines and habits themselves for writing and prayer isn't the point. We aren't trying to force God to reward our self-discipline. We aren't owed anything by readers when we write, no matter how sincere or vulnerable we are. There aren't "measurable outcomes" or clear road maps that show us where these practices will lead us. We're simply creating space for prayer and writing to flourish. Whether we start by creating space to pray and write or continually take stock of our fears and struggles through personal maintenance practices, we are always living by faith.

Living by faith shouldn't feel safe. It should feel a bit wild and reckless. Our society loves safe bets, investments with guaranteed returns, and systems that can never fail. We're trained to seek out the careers that are most likely to provide ample job opportunities, lucrative salaries, and gratifying returns on our investments in education. While I'm not bashing a secure or stable job, it's worth noting that our culture has essentially programmed us to not live by faith. We've been told to avoid the unknown.

Writing and prayer are both hopeful leaps into the darkness.

We're stepping into uncharted territory, and we could very well uncover something that could turn our lives upside down. We can't always control the words that come together on the page. Sometimes we just instinctively know what works, and "what works" may push the limits of our comfort. By the same token, we can't control the direction of prayer. While I firmly believe that prayer can lead us to greater comfort and peace, it's also a highly disruptive practice. The majority of the stories in the Bible that involve God providing direction to people resulted in them taking difficult and sometimes risky steps.

Taking a leap of faith into prayer and writing requires redefining failure and success. Sometimes helping readers isn't the surest way to high sales or income. Perhaps we'll appear foolish or wasteful if we press on with a mission to help others rather than writing for the largest audience. The same goes for my own Christian culture that obsessively measures how many people have decided to follow Christ at an event or how many new members have joined a church in a year in order to measure impact, success, and, heaven forbid, the approval of God.

If you're growing as a writer, then you are succeeding. Thankfully, it's not that hard to grow as a writer. You just need to make time to actually write as often as possible, learn new things when you can, and take some risks.

If you're creating space in your day to pray and meet with God, then you are succeeding. The more you open yourself to God, the deeper you will go in prayer.

Stop looking at numbers. Numbers can be manipulated. Numbers change. Numbers lie. Numbers don't offer any lasting meaning.

This is a shift in mindset. It may take a lot of practice. It may even feel like you're lying to yourself. Perhaps you need to fail at the numbers game first.

The numbers game will wear you out and let you down. Even if you can win at the numbers game for a little while, you'll eventually burn out and wonder what exactly you've gained.

Growing deeper into the disciplines of prayer and writing together will help you do both sustainably over the long term. Every writer I know who plans to write for the long term adopts something that resembles the disciplines of personal maintenance I've mentioned in this book. They pay attention to their surroundings, body, mind, and spirit. They recognize when they need to step back from a project or social media tool. They recognize when they are running out of energy. They stop and reevaluate their plans. Among the many Christian writers I know, prayer is intimately tied into their writing work. Many times their projects begin while praying or sitting in silence. The silence they cultivate in prayer gives their minds valuable rest before diving back into writing.

Everything is connected. Prayer and writing intersect and grow together because they use many of the same disciplines. What we pray about often provides something to write about, and what we write about often provides something to pray about. They create a self-sustaining circle. However, we can't begin that cycle without faith. We have to stop ourselves, look ahead into the unknown void before us, and jump.

We have to stop our housework or turn off the television to pray.

We have to stop running errands or scrolling through social media so that we actually start writing.

I can't guarantee results right away. It may take a while. You may need to ask a friend for guidance if you're struggling to pray or write. The results may not be what you expect.

If you're committed to prayer and writing, then you can begin with both in the same place: a blank. You begin prayer with empty hands and writing with a white page. You begin with expectation, promise, and hope. You begin with faith that committing to prayer and writing, especially together, will lead you to something. It's my hope and prayer that the *something* you find is a gift that changes your life and you can share that gift with others.

There's no mystery here about where to begin. Download the Examine app, schedule a time to pray or write in a quiet room without interruptions, take a walk with a small notebook or notes app handy, look up the Divine Hours online, turn off your internet and open a blank document, or wake up 30 minutes early to journal a few pages. If anything, there are too many paths forward. The good news is that you just need to start with one. Let it guide you. Build on your success, and continue adding more space for more practices as you see ideas and prayers spring to life. Pray, write, grow. Write, pray, grow. It doesn't matter what you do first. At a certain point, you'll see that they're often the same exact thing.

Thanks for Reading!

You're Invited to Join My Community of Readers

You can get TWO FREE eBooks, first dibs (as well as discounts) on new book releases, and learn about my other books by signing up for my e-newsletter.

Visit <u>www.edcyzewski.com</u> to sign up today!

What Did You Think of *Pray, Write, Grow*?

Can you take a moment to leave a brief review at a major reading site like <u>Amazon</u> or <u>Goodreads</u>? Your review will help readers know if they should give this book a shot, and I'd be grateful if you took a few minutes to do this!

About the Author

Ed Cyzewski writes at www.edcyzewski.com where his love for prayer, writing, and bad puns come together. He is the author of *A Path to Publishing*, *Coffeehouse Theology*, *A Christian Survival Guide*, and many other books on Christianity and creativity. He is a graduate of Biblical Theological Seminary, avid gardener, and devotee to New York style pizza.

GETTING STARTED

Visit www.edcyzewski.com/pwg to find clickable links for many of the resources in the lists that follow.

Writing Quick Start Guide

Writing Tips and Prompt

While I'm personally not a huge fan of writing tips or prompts, there are a few simple practices that can help you cut through the challenges you face. Here are some common tips I share with authors in coaching calls and emails:

- Learn to recognize when you are stressed, tired, or distracted. Pay attention to what drains your creative energy. For instance, do online arguments or news reports rob you of creative energy? Avoid social media when its time to be mentally present for a writing project.
- Work with scraps, half-baked ideas, and outlines in a journal. Be prepared to jot something down at all times. You'll only use some of these scraps. That's OK.
- A free write in a single journal page or a small blog project can provide a "small win" at the start of your writing time. It may be easier to begin a big project after you've hit a small goal.
- When working on a larger book project, I often begin a

new day by reviewing at least part of the previous day's work. It helps me get into the mindset required for the project and helps me write with better continuity from day to day.

- Embrace the process. Outline, draft, delete, edit, marinate, and edit again. Every writer needs several drafts before writing something good.
- Face the big questions, deep struggles, and biggest fears in your life when you journal. You don't have to share what you write. This kind of writing can lead you to your best prayers and your best work.
- Waking up early to write is essential for me. The afternoon is where good writing goes to die.

Resources
- Bird by Bird: Some Instructions on Writing and Life by Anne Lamott
- The Maker's Schedule
- The Art of Keeping a Journal via The Art of Simple blog
- Zen Habits (www.zenhabits.net)
- 20 Rules for Writing from Famous Writers in Writers Digest
- Why Walking Helps Us Think in The New Yorker
- Stephen King's 20 Rules for Writers
- David Foster Wallace's Mind-Blog Creative Nonfiction Syllabus
- Good Prose: The Art of Nonfiction by Tracy Kidder and Richard Todd
- The War of Art: Break Through the Blocks and Win Your Inner Creative Battles by Steven Pressfield
- Manage Your Day-to-Day: Build Your Routine, Find Your Focus, and Sharpen Your Creative Mind by Jocelyn K. Glei
- Zen in the Art of Writing: Essays in Creativity by Ray Bradbury
- The Power of Habit: Why We Do What We Do in Life and Business by Charles Duhigg
- Learning to Walk without an Agenda by Emily Freeman

Prayer Quick Start Guide

Prayer Practices
If you aren't sure where to begin with prayer, try one or several of the prayer practices listed below.

- Rituals and schedules help us pray. The monks were onto something! Try setting aside one period of time every day as your prayer time. Even if it's five minutes each morning, you'll soon miss it if you start skipping it.
- Use The Divine Hours for Daily scripture reading. Block out short pieces of time and let the readings guide your prayers.
- Look into the practice of Lectio Divina that slowly reads through a small passage of scripture as a means of entering into prayer. I often use a reading from the Hours to meditate on scripture.
- Set aside short blocks of time for silent prayer. The "Examine" app for iOS is ideal for reflection on the negative and positive elements of each day. It also prompts you to take five minutes for meditation. You can also find Examen guides online (Note that the two spellings sometimes interchange).
- Practice awareness of your mind and body throughout the day. What are you dwelling on while washing the dishes, driving, etc. Can you create space for your mind to be still, such as turning off the radio or television? What is your body telling you about your mental or spiritual state? Is your body communicating through pain, especially in your neck and shoulders?

Resources
- Immortal Diamond: The Search for Our True Self by Richard Rohr
- Daily Meditations from Richard Rohr (Mostly book excerpts)
- Richard Rohr on Super Soul Sunday
- The Examine App
- Examen questions from IVP

- Ignatian Spirituality page on the examen
- Ignatian guide to prayer
- The Divine Hours at Ann Arbor Vineyard's website
- On Prayer by Thomas Keating (An introduction to centering prayer)
- The Jesus Prayer (An Orthodox guide)
- An Introduction to Lectio Divina
- How Everything We Tell Ourselves about How Busy We Are Is a Lie
- The End of Absence: Reclaiming What We've Lost in a World of Constant Connection

AFTERWORD

This book first took shape while co-leading a retreat that focused on prayer and writing called Renew and Refine with my friend Kristin Tennant. I have long noticed how writing and prayer work together, and there's nothing like planning a retreat for a small group of Christian writers to focus your thinking! I developed these ideas further during a "Writer's Circle" at the Festival of Faith and Writing. Throughout the past two years, Kristin and our many friends who attended the retreat and our writer's circle have been crucial conversation partners in the development of the ideas in this book.

I'm always grateful for the feedback of my social media friends and followers, as well as my blog and e-newsletter readers who provided feedback in the early stages of this project. What you shared and commented on helped guide me in the early stages and I can't thank you enough for the time each of you took to read my work along the way. Special thanks to Tanya Marlow, Melissa Gutierrez, and Mary Beth Pavlik.

I mentioned Anne Lamott as an influence in the introduction, but I also couldn't have written this book with the same level of clarity if it hadn't been for the work of Richard Rohr. I'm a subscriber to his daily newsletter and have found it a lifeline each week. I also read his books <u>Immortal Diamond</u> and <u>Everything Belongs</u> while working on this project and would recommend both for anyone interested in writing or prayer.

Lastly, I want to dedicate this book to my writer friends who are committed to serving others with their words, who recognize all of the unhealthy aspects of the publishing industry, and who write from a place of prayerful authenticity. You give me hope, and I pray that my words do the same for you.

- Ed Cyzewski

ALSO BY ED CYZEWSKI

Books for Writers
Creating Space: The Case for Everyday Creativity
A Path to Publishing: What I Learned by Publishing a Nonfiction
Book

Christian Living Books
A Christian Survival Guide: A Lifeline to Faith and Growth
Why We Run from God's Love
Unfollowers: Unlikely Lessons on Faith from Those Who Doubted
Jesus
The Good News of Revelation
Hazardous: Committing to the Cost of Following Jesus
Divided We Unite: Practical Christian Unity
Coffeehouse Theology: Reflecting on God in Everyday Life

Visit Ed's blog for samples and ordering info:
http://edcyzewski.com/my-books/

A Path to Publishing: What I Learned by Publishing a Nonfiction Book
(2014, Revised Edition)

A Path to Publishing is a big-picture, step-by-step guide for nonfiction publishing hopefuls. Beginning with mental preparation for writing and building a platform, Cyzewski helps readers develop their ideas, write regularly, pitch a proposal, and market their work. Through accounts of his experiences, a series of case studies, and action steps, each chapter moves readers toward the final goal of becoming published writers.

Creating Space: The Case for Everyday Creativity

Creativity is a gift everyone has been given to share, but doubt, discouragement, and distractions hinder the ability of many to pursue their creative passions. Creating Space advocates for the creative gifts in every person, arguing that...

- Creativity is not a mistake.
- Creativity can be developed.
- Creativity is a vitally important gift for others.

This brief manifesto on creativity is for everyone. Whether you doodle, sing in the shower, knit scarves, or scribble poems, Creating Space will encourage you to make space in your life in order to fulfill your creative calling, using your gifts to their fullest extent.

Unfollowers: Unlikely Lessons on Faith from Those Who Doubted Jesus
Ed Cyzewski and Derek Cooper

Unfollowers re-tells the Gospels from the perspectives of those who ignored or opposed Jesus, asking the question: What can followers of Jesus learn from the dropouts, detractors, and doubters of the Gospels? Their stories guide us in overcoming common obstacles to discipleship and remind us that following

Jesus is often counter-intuitive and surprising.

The Good News of Revelation
Ed Cyzewski and Larry Helyer

The original readers of Revelation had a very different experience of John's letter compared to the fear and anxiety that grips readers today. John intended his letter to encourage seven suffering churches to persevere as they waited for Christ's return. Rather than detailing a rapture that escapes suffering, Revelation has a message about suffering, good vs. evil, and the justice of God that is relevant for John's audience and readers today.

A Christian Survival Guide: A Lifeline to Faith and Growth

A Christian Survival Guide uses humor and straightforward, biblical answers to help life-long Christians and new believers grow in their relationships with God by tackling the tough questions and common pitfalls in Christian belief and practice. Rather than permitting persistent sin and lingering doubts to hold them back from God, Christians can shore up their faith by getting the basics of Christianity straight, and moving into a thriving relationship with God, even if every question isn't answered. Readers will be encouraged to run the race of faith in order to win--albeit with a cramp from a good laugh.

Coffeehouse Theology: Reflecting on God in Everyday Life

Coffeehouse Theology will help readers understand, shape, and live out their beliefs. Beginning with a discussion about the ways cultural context impacts theology, Coffeehouse Theology roots theology in the church's mission to be the presence of God's Kingdom. Far from dividing the church, theology unites the church in a dynamic dialogue about the presence of God, his revelation in scripture, and the interpretations of the historic and global churches.

Hazardous: Committing to the Cost of Following Jesus
Ed Cyzewski and Derek Cooper

Hazardous encourages disciples of Jesus to count the steep costs of following Jesus in their daily lives by equipping them to pursue holiness, listen for God's guidance, and obey God's direction. A lot of books tell us that discipleship is costly, but this book shows what it looks like and how God helps us persevere in the midst of trials.

Visit Ed's blog for more info:
http://edcyzewski.com/my-books/

PREVIEW

CREATING SPACE

The Case for Everyday Creativity

:: why create? ::

One day everything in my life changed.

My wife napped nearby in her hospital bed. I sat across the room looking at Ethan, our newborn son, in his crib next to her. With her graduate school schedule and his needs, I began to wonder if I'd ever find the time to write.

I mean, I knew I'd still "write." However, it was one thing to write for businesses to help pay our bills. I knew that would continue.

I began to worry about my blog, the websites I write for, and all of my book projects that were under consideration with editors at that time. How would I ever find time for it all?

In that moment, I made a simple resolution. During the first two weeks of Ethan's life, I would write at least one page in my journal. I'd be on paternity leave. I had colleagues covering my business clients, and I'd lined up guest posts for my blog.

I didn't "have" to write.

Nevertheless, I had this nagging notion that I needed to write at this point in my life more than ever. I needed writing to be as much a part of my life as I needed Ethan. I didn't want my creativity to wither as I poured myself into him.

As I sat down to write in the hospital that evening and in the days that followed, I gained a sense of clarity about the role of creativity in my life and in the lives of others.

Coming from the American Christian tradition, I tend to focus on the practical things of life. Whether that's the overly spiritual "saving souls" becoming the highest goal or the grounded Christian left that makes "fighting poverty" the holiest of callings, I've struggled to find a place for my creativity.

How could I justify taking time to write stories when there were so many needs, both physical and spiritual, in our world?

Faced with the potential annihilation of my creativity with a newborn in my arms and the guilt of my religion on my shoulders, I found myself clinging to writing desperately. Something in my spirit latched onto that journal and pen with a tenacity that nearly knocked me out of my chair.

Following that moment of revelation, I began to write about why I need to create and why others need to create as well. In fact, I believe all of us have some kind of creative spark that needs to be protected and fueled. That spark may come to life in our day jobs, in our moments at home with our kids, or in the quiet of the evening when those around us slumber.

What follows is the fleshed out version of those journal entries.

This is a call, an invitation, a challenge, and a shove to let your creative gifts come to life and to sustain them.

I don't use the word "gifts" lightly. We have been given creativity for a reason. We nurture it because creativity has been woven into the fabric of our world. Whether you believe that's by divine design or by random chance, the place of creativity in our world is unmistakable.

The hard part is believing that you hold a piece of that puzzle.

You need to create because there is a part of you that is meant to come alive when you're at the computer, behind a piano, holding a pen, or handling a needle.

You need to create because once you embrace your creativity you'll have gifts to share with your community.

You need to create because even if everything around you changes, your gifts don't.

□

:: sandcastles ::

I used to build sandcastles each summer at the beach. These weren't little outposts with a turret or two. My cousins and I built enormous walls, towers, and moats. It took all day, with the building crew only pausing for a few quick dips in the ocean.

We usually finished the building of the castle by destroying it with a plastic soldier battle. What we didn't finish ourselves was swept away that evening by the tide.

Each day we returned to a smooth spot on the beach, a white canvas waiting for our imaginations to kick into gear. We lugged water or clumps of wet sand back to our spot and set to work, joyful that we could spend an entire day sculpting, even though our materials were little more than fragile and impermanent sand.

Every time I see a plastic sandcastle mold, I become a child again in my mind, sitting on the beach with my cousins, carefully constructing a new fortress. There are few fonder memories from my childhood than those sandcastles, even if they only lasted for a few hours at the most in their finished state.

There was a simple joy about creating back then. The act itself was its own reward. I wouldn't trade anything for that experience.

At a certain point in our lives, we were told that creating isn't practical, efficient, or responsible. We need to get the laundry done, cook dinner, clean the house, pick up after the kids, work long hours, pay the bills, and tackle a thousand other responsibilities.

Who has the time to be creative? Who would be foolish enough to invest untold hours into making something beautiful and long lasting? You can just pick up something similar on the cheap at the store and rush home to... watch television?

In our quest for efficiency and productivity, we have lost the joy of creating.
• Meals are prepackaged.
• Mass-produced household items cram shelves at box stores.
• Everyone picks up the same art at IKEA.

Creativity is for kids and a few artistic types.

More often than not, the "artistic types" are viewed as kids who never figured out the need for a "real job" or who shun the responsibilities of real life.

I'm not going to argue that reintroducing creativity into your life is more efficient. It's not. It's slow, sometimes painful, and always comes with a cost.

Whether or not it's convenient or efficient, creativity is healthy and necessary. Some kind of creativity has been hard-wired into all of us. It's aching to come out of you.

It's time to let it come to life.

Thanks for Reading This Preview!

Download the rest of Creating Space from Amazon.com or other eBook sellers.

31275737R00058

Made in the USA
San Bernardino, CA
05 March 2016